Explorer Hat: to keep the sun away... and look cool

Flashlight: helps me see in the dark

Backpack: keeps all my gear and a snack (just in case)

Erlenmeyer Flask: is great for mixing liquids (or chemicals) without spilling

Petri Dish: for growing tiny things like bacteria

Bunsen Burner: so I can see what happens to stuff when it gets really hot

Telescope: to look at stars and planets that are very very very far away.

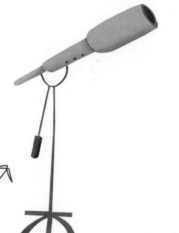

Rock Pick: to break apart big rocks and make little rocks.

Net: essential for catching butterflies

Rain Boots: keep my feet clean so I don't bring mud in the house + they're stylish

Meet Einstein

illustrated by
Viviana Garofoli

written by
Mariela Kleiner

MB*

Meet Books, LLC

"Imagination is more important than knowledge."
~ Albert Einstein

Meet Einstein
Text copyright © 2011 by Mariela Kleiner
Illustrations copyright © 2011 by Viviana Garofoli

Published by Meet Books, LLC in the United States
Printed in China

For information regarding permission, please contact:
Meet Books, LLC. 806 Seale Avenue, Palo Alto, California 94303
meeteinstein@gmail.com
www.MeetEinstein.com

Library of Congress Control Number: 2009908521
ISBN 978-0-615-38973-8

Book design by Mariela Kleiner

For Hailey and Ethan, who inspire me everyday.
To Keith, my resident scientist (and IT guy).
— M.K.

To Julieta, Nahuel and Juan Cruz
— V.G.

Meet Albert Einstein. He is a scientist.

Scientists study the Earth and the sky.

They also study animals,

plants,

and even our bodies!

Scientists like to ask lots of questions

Why do we plug things into the wall?

What makes a kite move around in the sky?

about why things happen and how things work.

What things do
plants need to
grow?

How do animals
talk to
each other?

Scientists
make lots of
discoveries

Einstein discovered
many new things
about light.

Light comes from the Sun.

Light also comes from a flashlight, lightbulbs, and fire.

Light can appear in all different colors, such as:

White Lights
(perfect for reading a book)

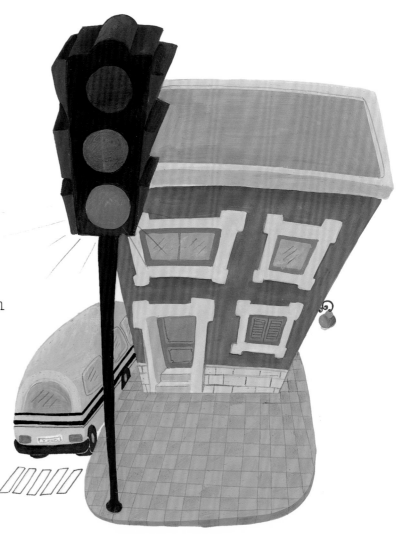

Green Lights
(tell us when its our turn to cross an intersection)

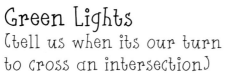

Red Lights
(shows us when
a car is stopping)

...And Even Rainbow Lights!
(find them on a wall, a bubble,
or up in the sky after a rain storm)

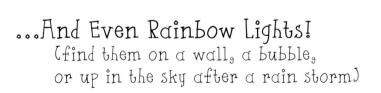

Einstein also discovered new things about gravity.

Gravity is the reason why things fall down to the ground.

When food spills from the table, it always falls down and not up.

When you
jump
high up
in the air
you always
come back
down
to the
ground.

Gravity keeps the Earth near the Sun,
so that the Sun can come up every morning...

and go down every night.

It also keeps the Moon up in the sky at night.

Isn't that cool?
You can think about Einstein next time you turn off the lights,
or watch something fall down to the ground.

And maybe one day you will be a scientist too.

Meet Einstein

for parents

About Albert Einstein:

- Einstein was born in Germany on March 14, 1879.

- He is famous for his theory of relativity, the dual wave particle theory of light, mass-energy equivalence ($E=mc^2$), and many other scientific discoveries.

- The dual wave particle theory: Einstein discovered that light is made up of tiny particles of energy called photons. Prior to Einstein, scientists generally classified light as an energy wave, but he discovered that light is both a wave and a particle. Einstein's theory of the dual nature of light paved the way for the entire field of quantum mechanics, which created a revolution in science.

- Einstein's Theory of Relativity: In 1915 Einstein published his general theory of relativity, which was a completely new way of explaining the fundamentals of gravity. It combined the three dimensions of space with time to create what is called space-time. Einstein's theory allowed for scientists to account for gravity more accurately, and therefore, it became crucial to future advancements in science.

- Mass-Energy Equivalence: Einstein is most famous for his equation $E=mc^2$. It states that the mass of an object is actually a measure of its energy content.

- In 1921 he received the Nobel Prize for his services to Theoretical Physics.

- Time magazine named him "Person of the Century" in 1999.

- Einstein died on April 17, 1955 at the age of 76. His remains were cremated and his ashes were scattered.

- Before the cremation, Princeton Hospital pathologist Thomas Stoltz Harvey removed Einstein's brain for preservation in hopes that the neuroscience of the future would discover what made Einstein so smart.

Reference: "Albert Einstein," Wikipedia, Jan 2009, <http://en.wikipedia.org/wiki/Albert_Einstein>.

Questions to ask your kids:

1. Are you a scientist too? Do you ask lots of questions?

2. Where do you see light everyday? How many different colors of light can you find?

3. Is light hot or cold?

4. Did you see something fall down today because of gravity?

5. Can you jump really high before gravity makes you come back down?

6. What things don't fall down to the floor when you drop them? (ex: a balloon, a kite)

7. What science tools do you use?

Interesting facts...

How can we see rainbow lights: White light is made up of all the colors we see in a rainbow. When white light splits up through refraction on a bubble, the side of a mirror, or a drop of water, we can see a rainbow.

Why gravity keeps the moon up in the sky: The moon travels at a high speed and wants to go in a direction away from the Earth, but gravity continually pulls it toward the Earth. The combination of gravity and the speed of the moon cause it to have a circular path around the Earth.

Stop Watch: to keep track of time

Notebook + Pen: so I don't forget what I notice or see

Binoculars: so I can see things that are really far away

Lab coat: so I don't get my clothes dirty

Microscope: to look at itty-bitty stuff

Gloves: protect my fingers from sticky and icky things

Books: so I can look stuff up and learn new things

Goggles: protect my eyes

Thermometer: to see how hot something is

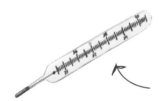

Ruler: to see how long things are

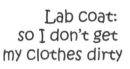

Balance: so I can test if one thing is heavier than another

Beakers: pretty glass jars that keep all my liquids (or chemicals) for experiments